# REFRESH

A Guided Sabbath Journal

This journal concept is dedicated to Savannah, Alice, and Sammi for challenging me in exploring the Sabbath with curious and gracious hearts.

# WHAT IS THE SABBATH?

*"Remember the Sabbath day, to keep it Holy. Six days you shall labor, and do all your work, but the seventh day is a Sabbath to the Lord your God…"- Exodus 20:8-10 (ESV)*

Most simply, Sabbath means rest or to cease from work. The Sabbath is a day devoted to resting in and with God, traditionally the seventh day of the week, following six days of work. There are people out in the world with more research on Sabbath than me, and who have more profound thoughts to inspire it. I didn't write this journal as an attempt to appear scholarly. I wrote this journal because God has changed my life through Sabbath, and therefore I know He can change yours too. The Sabbath is a practice and a discipline, asking us to slow down and be present. We are surrounded by a culture that screams, "IF YOU SLOW DOWN, YOU'LL BE LEFT BEHIND OR RAN OVER." Sabbath is counter-cultural, ancient, and holy. The Sabbath is a day dedicated to worshiping, communicating with, and just simply being with God.

Additionally, the Sabbath is a gift. I once received an all-access pass to my dance studio as a birthday gift. I went weeks without using it and finally found the time to go take a class. I knew in my heart it would fill my mind and body with the endorphins I needed to get through the week. I felt a little embarrassed showing up, knowing that my instructor would have noticed my absences, but she embraced me with open arms declaring, "My little Tinkerbell is back again, oh how joyful a day." I left the class full of delight and a little sore from stretching neglected muscles. My experience with the dance pass is a similar narrative to how many of us interact with the Sabbath. It is an all-access, free pass to an entire day with the one who knows our deepest needs and desires, the one who pursues us with an unfailing love, the one who truly renews and refreshes our soul. Yet, we make excuses as to why we can't or don't have time to spend a whole day devoted to this gift of Sabbath, this gift of time communing with God, resting our bodies and souls.

# WHO SHOULD SABBATH?

*"So then, there remains a Sabbath rest for the people of God, for whoever has entered God's rest has also rested from his works as God did from His."- Hebrews 4:9-10 (ESV)*

Before college, my assumption of the Sabbath was that it was something that people of Jewish faith and culture practiced. It wasn't until my small group began diving into how to pursue God deeper among our busy lives that I started to study the history and intent of a Sabbath day. So now, I would simply say that anyone who wants to experience fullness of rest, relationship with God, and desires to become more like Jesus should Sabbath. This feels easier said than done in certain seasons of life, but similarly to any spiritual discipline, it might just take some intentional and creative thought.

When talking to my friend Davis, I asked him about how his parents incorporated Sabbath while having children and busy lives. What he told me I believe will encourage busy families and stay-at-home parents alike. He said, "When they practiced Sabbath, we practiced Sabbath." Davis explained that growing up he knew that there was one day a week that they didn't make plans except to worship, be outside, and have closeness as a family following after God together. It was something that they chose to prioritize. When I was a college student and new to practicing Sabbath, I Sabbathed from 7pm on Wednesday to 3pm on Thursday because this was the most practical time for my work, school and ministry schedule. Although it wasn't a full 24 hours, it was still a sacred time that I held

dearly to be able to step away from everything and take a breath in solitude. Let me also encourage you, that you do not need to be at a certain part of your faith journey to qualify to practice Sabbath. The word Sabbath can sound intimidating and grandiose but it is truly available to everyone. Whether you are just starting to explore faith, or you have been a student of Jesus for 50 years, Sabbath rest is for you and you are invited by God today.

# WHY SHOULD WE SABBATH?

*"You shall keep my Sabbaths and reverence my sanctuary: I am the Lord."- Leviticus 26:2 (ESV)*

For one day, we offer our full availability to God. So often, we offer our schedule to our children, partner, community groups, friends, and careers. None of these are a bad place to set our attention, but they also will not fulfill our deepest needs and desires. These people and institutions often demand that we give them our full attention or there will be consequences. We believe that if we don't put everything into our career, we will lose it. We believe that if we don't spend every minute of high school studying, being the president of ASB or some other club, make varsity for a sport, we won't get into college. We believe that if we don't do that thing with our friends, we will grow distant. The list can go on and on. These are simply lies that the enemy tells us to divert our attention away from God and onto the world. We can only give fully to others when we are fulfilled by and full of the Spirit ourselves. We must work *from* our rest, not work *for* our rest. We should Sabbath in humility as worship unto our heavenly Father, to prepare for the week ahead, and to prevent mental and physical exhaustion.

When we are exhausted we are the most vulnerable for attack. Our immune system becomes weak and we are prone to illness; our body becomes tired and unable to function in basic ways. But it's not just physical, it's mental too. With mental and emotional exhaustion, we can often feel it is more difficult to focus and have a harder time processing and controlling our emotions. Finally, we see it so evidently as the enemy attacks us spiritually when we are exhausted. When we don't take the opportunity to Sabbath, we lose precious time with our greatest pursuer and become more susceptible to guilt, shame and other tactics the enemy uses to distance us from God. We should Sabbath because our God desires a relationship with us and we experience fullness of joy in His presence! We feel physically, mentally, and spiritually renewed after we Sabbath. What better way is there to start a new week?

# WHAT SHOULD I DO ON MY SABBATH?

*"It is good to give thanks to the Lord, to sing praises to your name, O Most High; to declare your steadfast love in the morning, and your faithfulness by night, to the music of the lute and the harp, to the melody of the lyre. For you, O Lord, have made me glad by your work; at the works of your hands I sing for joy."- Psalm 92: 1-4 (ESV)*

Every person's Sabbath will look different. I heard it said by pastor Matt Chandler that "those who work with their hands, Sabbath with their minds. Those who work with their minds Sabbath with their hands." Personally, I have found this guidance to be true in my practice! When I worked as a barista, my body was exhausted, so my Sabbaths were heavy in reading and stillness. Now that I work in the legal field, my Sabbaths are much more physically energetic with dance classes and long walks.

I have developed five "pillars" that I try to incorporate into my practice each week. These pillars and ideas are by no means 'one size fits all'; they are just some inspirations of how to spend your time intentionally drawing nearer to God. Be open, give your expectations over to the Lord, and ask him to inspire your unique day. If you feel overwhelmed by the idea of taking a whole day, start small. Block off 2-3 hours for your first few Sabbaths, and go from there. I promise, once you start, you won't want to stop. I also encourage you to turn off your phone for the majority of the day to avoid distractions and best allow yourself to be present. I usually text my parents and a few close friends to let them know my phone will be off for "x" amount of

time. I let them know where I will be going, and what time to expect to hear from me later. This keeps me safe and lets them know why they may not get a hold of me. Now without further ado, here's some jumping off points.

# MY FIVE PILLARS OF SABBATH

### *Prayer*
- Go on a prayer walk and allow space to listen
- Write prayers on sticky notes to put on your wall
- Keep a prayer journal

### *Creativity*
- Try out a new recipe to cook or bake
- Paint a canvas
- Dance

### *Worship*
- Go for a drive and sing through a worship playlist
- Say gratitudes while stretching
- Acts of service or volunteering

### *Learning*
- Listen to a podcast
- Watch a "The Bible Project" video
- Dive into scripture

### *Reflection*
- Draw a word map describing your last week
- Process what you're learning or experiencing with a friend
- Fill out your Refresh journal

# HOW DO I USE THE JOURNAL?

Before jumping into your journal pages each week I would encourage you to pray something similar to the following: "Heavenly Father, thank you for meeting me here today, as I am. I pray you slow down my mind and help to keep me grounded in your presence, uninterrupted by my own distractions. Guide me to see how you are intentionally pursuing me in this season. Through Scripture, reveal to me pieces of your character, goodness and sovereignty so I may know you more deeply. Thank you for this time and I pray your Spirit guides my Sabbath day. Amen."
Remember, the exact words or length of your prayer isn't what's important. What's important is setting your heart with intention and opening yourself to God.

Now onto the journal…

The left hand side page has a Psalm at the top, followed by a lined journal page for reflection and application. Why Psalms as the scripture focus? Throughout 2020, I did my best to read a Psalm each night. I connected deeply to the honest mix of lament and praise. Similar to David and the other Psalmists, I wrestled with grief and fear, but also found joy in God's presence and hope in his promises. Like the Psalms, I wanted the journal to be a space where hard questions could be asked, prayers would be answered, and love would lead in abundance.

On the right hand page side you will see three headings with free-form spaces. I have provided some example prompts below that can be used as jumping off points in these sections. The first section, "Rejoice", is a space led by gratitude. "Rejoice" seeks acknowledgment of God showing up, even if we are moving too fast to see it. The second area, "Reflect", is also looking back at the past week, but this section is meant to be more introspective than the first, with questions prompting us to look inside ourselves. Finally, "Reach" looks forward to the next week and asks questions about how we can be more intentional in our thoughts and actions as we go about our days. Since this section is free-form, feel free to draw, word map, journal, or use the space in another creative way. Once you get the hang of it, start writing your own questions too, but until then I've written some examples below!

### Rejoice
- When did I experience God's kindness and grace?
- Where did I see beauty in creation?
- What prayer did God answer or address?

### Reflect
- When did I elevate faith over fear?
- What lie am I believing that needs to be replaced with biblical truth?
- Who do I need to forgive or ask for forgiveness from?

### Reach
- What comfort could I sacrifice to pursue Jesus more? (Screen time, fasting, etc.)
- Who can I serve intentionally this week?
- Which fruit of the spirit will I focus on this week?

And with that, I leave you to be led by the Spirit in your Sabbath rest.

# NUACH

Just as He pursues me, so too
must I rest
and revere the sanctity
of a Lord that permits me the peace
the pause
the permission
to seek His voice in silence
and solitude.
To shut away worldly things
and reset my mind on things above.
Casting my cares
and my worries
and my anxieties
on Him
for he commands me so.
Because to search for calm in the chaos
is victory. For even God
found respite from his own creation
and the universe expanded
in gratitude.

*- Rachel LaBrasca*

## PSALM 3:4-5

*"I cried aloud to the Lord, and he answered me from his holy hill. I lay down and slept: I woke again, for the Lord sustained me."*

# REJOICE

# REFLECT

# REACH

WHAT REFRESHED
MY SOUL TODAY?

## PSALM 5:11-12

*"But let all who take refuge in you rejoice; let them ever sing for you, and spread your protection over them, that those who love your name may exult in you. For you bless the righteous, O Lord; you cover him with favor as with a shield."*

# REJOICE

# REFLECT

# REACH

WHAT REFRESHED
MY SOUL TODAY?

## PSALM 6:2-3

*"Be gracious to me, O Lord, for I am languishing; heal me, O Lord, for my bones are troubled. My soul also is greatly troubled. But you, O Lord—how long?"*

# REJOICE

# REFLECT

# REACH

WHAT REFRESHED
MY SOUL TODAY?

*"The Lord is a stronghold for the oppressed, a stronghold in times of trouble. And those who know your name put their trust in you, for you, O Lord, have not forsaken those who seek you."*

# REJOICE

# REFLECT

# REACH

WHAT REFRESHED
MY SOUL TODAY?

## PSALM 16:8-11

*"I have set the Lord always before me; because he is at my right hand, I shall not be shaken. Therefore my heart is glad, and my whole being rejoices; my flesh also dwells secure. For you will not abandon my soul to Sheol, or let your holy one see corruption. You make known to me the path of life; in your presence there is fullness of joy; at your right hand are pleasures forevermore."*

# REJOICE

# REFLECT

# REACH

WHAT REFRESHED
MY SOUL TODAY?

## PSALM 18:1-3

*"I love you, O Lord, my strength. The Lord is my rock and my fortress and my deliverer, my God, my rock, in whom I take refuge, my shield, and the horn of my salvation, my stronghold. I call upon the Lord, who is worthy to be praised, and I am saved from my enemies."*

## REJOICE

## REFLECT

## REACH

WHAT REFRESHED
MY SOUL TODAY?

## PSALM 23:1-4

*"The Lord is my shepherd; I shall not want. He makes me lie down in green pastures. He leads me beside still waters. He restores my soul. He leads me in paths of righteousness for his name's sake. Even though I walk through the valley of the shadow of death, I will fear no evil, for you are with me; your rod and your staff, they comfort me."*

REJOICE

REFLECT

REACH

WHAT REFRESHED
MY SOUL TODAY?

*"You prepare a table before me in the presence of my enemies; you anoint my head with oil; my cup overflows. Surely goodness and mercy shall follow me all the days of my life, and I shall dwell in the house of the Lord forever."*

# REJOICE

# REFLECT

# REACH

WHAT REFRESHED
MY SOUL TODAY?

*"The Lord is my light and my salvation; whom shall I fear? The Lord is the stronghold of my life; of whom shall I be afraid?"*

# REJOICE

# REFLECT

# REACH

WHAT REFRESHED
MY SOUL TODAY?

## PSALM 27:13-14

*"I believe that I shall look upon the goodness of the Lord in the land of the living! Wait for the Lord; be strong, and let your heart take courage; wait for the Lord!"*

# REJOICE

# REFLECT

# REACH

WHAT REFRESHED
MY SOUL TODAY?

## PSALM 32:10

*"Many are the sorrows of the wicked, but steadfast love surrounds the one who trusts in the Lord."*

# REJOICE

# REFLECT

# REACH

WHAT REFRESHED
MY SOUL TODAY?

## PSALM 34:5

*"Those who look to him are radiant, and their faces shall never be ashamed."*

# REJOICE

# REFLECT

# REACH

WHAT REFRESHED
MY SOUL TODAY?

*"When the righteous cry for help, the Lord hears and delivers them out of all their troubles. The Lord is near to the brokenhearted and saves the crushed in spirit. Many are the afflictions of the righteous, but the Lord delivers him out of them all."*

# REJOICE

# REFLECT

# REACH

WHAT REFRESHED
MY SOUL TODAY?

# PSALM 37:30

*"The mouth of the righteous utters wisdom, and his tongue speaks justice."*

# REJOICE

# REFLECT

# REACH

WHAT REFRESHED
MY SOUL TODAY?

*"I waited patiently for the Lord; he inclined to me and heard my cry. He drew me up from the pit of destruction, out of the miry bog, and set my feet upon a rock, making my steps secure."*

# REJOICE

# REFLECT

# REACH

WHAT REFRESHED
MY SOUL TODAY?

# PSALM 42:1-2

*"As a deer pants for flowing streams, so pants my soul for you, O God. My soul thirsts for God, for the living God. When shall I come and appear before God?"*

# REJOICE

# REFLECT

# REACH

WHAT REFRESHED
MY SOUL TODAY?

## PSALM 42:11

*"Why are you cast down, O my soul, and why are you in turmoil within me? Hope in God; for I shall again praise him, my salvation and my God."*

# REJOICE

# REFLECT

# REACH

WHAT REFRESHED
MY SOUL TODAY?

## PSALM 43:3

*"Send out your light and your truth; let them lead me; let them bring me to your holy hill and to your dwelling!"*

# REJOICE

# REFLECT

# REACH

WHAT REFRESHED
MY SOUL TODAY?

*"God is our refuge and strength, a very present help in trouble. Therefore we will not fear though the earth gives way, though the mountains be moved into the heart of the sea, though its waters roar and foam, though the mountains tremble at its swelling."*

# REJOICE

# REFLECT

# REACH

WHAT REFRESHED
MY SOUL TODAY?

*"My mouth shall speak wisdom; the meditation of my heart shall be understanding."*

# REJOICE

# REFLECT

# REACH

WHAT REFRESHED
MY SOUL TODAY?

## PSALM 51:10

*"Create in me a clean heart, O God, and renew a right spirit within me."*

# REJOICE

# REFLECT

# REACH

WHAT REFRESHED
MY SOUL TODAY?

# PSALM 55:16-17

*"But I call to God, and the Lord will save me. Evening and morning and at noon I utter my complaint and moan and he hears my voice."*

# REJOICE

# REFLECT

# REACH

WHAT REFRESHED
MY SOUL TODAY?

# PSALM 56:8

*"You have kept count of my tossings; put my tears in your bottle. Are they not in your book?"*

# REJOICE

# REFLECT

# REACH

WHAT REFRESHED
MY SOUL TODAY?

## PSALM 61:1-3

*"Hear my cry, O God, listen to my prayer, from the end of the earth I call to you when my heart is faint. Lead me to the rock that is higher than I, for you have been my refuge, a strong tower against the enemy."*

# REJOICE

# REFLECT

# REACH

WHAT REFRESHED
MY SOUL TODAY?

## PSALM 62:5-6

*"For God alone, O my soul, wait in silence, for my hope is from him. He only is my rock and my salvation, my fortress; I shall not be shaken."*

# REJOICE

# REFLECT

# REACH

WHAT REFRESHED
MY SOUL TODAY?

*"Whom have I in heaven but you? And there is nothing on earth that I desire besides you. My flesh and my heart may fail, but God is the strength of my heart and my portion forever."*

# REJOICE

# REFLECT

# REACH

WHAT REFRESHED
MY SOUL TODAY?

# PSALM 73:28

*"But for me it is good to be near God; I have made the Lord God my refuge, that I may tell of all your works."*

# REJOICE

# REFLECT

# REACH

WHAT REFRESHED
MY SOUL TODAY?

*"I will remember the deeds of the Lord; yes, I will remember your wonders of old. I will ponder all your work, and meditate on your mighty deeds."*

# REJOICE

# REFLECT

# REACH

WHAT REFRESHED
MY SOUL TODAY?

PSALM 84:3-4

*"Even the sparrow finds a home, and the swallow a nest for herself, where she may lay her young, at your altars, O Lord of hosts, my King and my God. Blessed are those who dwell in your house, ever singing your praise!"*

# REJOICE

# REFLECT

# REACH

WHAT REFRESHED
MY SOUL TODAY?

*"Steadfast love and faithfulness meet; righteousness and peace kiss each other. Faithfulness springs up from the ground, and righteousness looks down from the sky."*

# REJOICE

# REFLECT

# REACH

WHAT REFRESHED
MY SOUL TODAY?

## PSALM 86:5-7

*"For you, O Lord, are good and forgiving, abounding in steadfast love to all who call upon you. Give ear, O Lord, to my prayer; listen to my plea for grace. In the day of my trouble I call upon you, for you answer me."*

# REJOICE

# REFLECT

# REACH

WHAT REFRESHED
MY SOUL TODAY?

# PSALM 88:2-3

*"Let my prayer come before you; incline your ear to my cry! For my soul is full of troubles, and my life draws near to Sheol."*

# REJOICE

# REFLECT

# REACH

WHAT REFRESHED
MY SOUL TODAY?

# PSALM 91:11

*"For he will command his angels concerning you to guard you in all your ways."*

# REJOICE

# REFLECT

# REACH

WHAT REFRESHED
MY SOUL TODAY?

*"When I thought, 'My foot slips,' your steadfast love, O Lord, held me up. When the cares of my heart are many, your consolations cheer my soul."*

# REJOICE

# REFLECT

# REACH

WHAT REFRESHED
MY SOUL TODAY?

## PSALM 100:4-5

*"Enter his gates with thanksgiving, and his courts with praise! Give thanks to him; bless his name! For the Lord is good; his steadfast love endures forever, and his faithfulness to all generations."*

# REJOICE

# REFLECT

# REACH

WHAT REFRESHED
MY SOUL TODAY?

## PSALM 103:11-12

*"For as high as the heavens are above the earth, so great is his steadfast love toward those who fear him; as far as the east is from the west, so far does he remove our transgressions from us."*

# REJOICE

# REFLECT

# REACH

WHAT REFRESHED
MY SOUL TODAY?

## PSALM 107:4-6

*"Some wandered in desert wastes, finding no way to a city to dwell in; hungry and thirsty, their soul fainted within them. Then they cried to the Lord in their trouble, and he delivered them from their distress."*

# REJOICE

# REFLECT

# REACH

WHAT REFRESHED
MY SOUL TODAY?

## PSALM 107:20-21

*"He sent out his word and healed them, and delivered them from their destruction. Let them thank the Lord for his steadfast love, for his wondrous works to the children of man!"*

# REJOICE

# REFLECT

# REACH

WHAT REFRESHED
MY SOUL TODAY?

"*Incline my heart to your testimonies, and not to selfish gain! Turn my eyes from looking at worthless things; and give me life in your ways.*"

# REJOICE

# REFLECT

# REACH

WHAT REFRESHED
MY SOUL TODAY?

## PSALM 121:7-8

*"The Lord will keep you from all evil; he will keep your life. The Lord will keep your going out and your coming in from this time forth and forevermore."*

# REJOICE

# REFLECT

# REACH

WHAT REFRESHED
MY SOUL TODAY?

## PSALM 127:2

*"It is in vain that you rise up early and go late to rest, eating the bread of anxious toil; for he gives to his beloved sleep."*

# REJOICE

# REFLECT

# REACH

WHAT REFRESHED
MY SOUL TODAY?

*"Out of the depths I cry to you, O Lord! O Lord, hear my voice! Let your ears be attentive to the voice of my pleas for mercy!"*

# REJOICE

# REFLECT

# REACH

WHAT REFRESHED
MY SOUL TODAY?

# PSALM 133:1

*"Behold, how good and pleasant it is when brothers dwell in unity!"*

# REJOICE

# REFLECT

# REACH

WHAT REFRESHED
MY SOUL TODAY?

# PSALM 136:16

*"To him who led his people through the wilderness, for his steadfast love endures forever."*

# REJOICE

# REFLECT

# REACH

WHAT REFRESHED
MY SOUL TODAY?

*"I bow down toward your holy temple and give thanks to your name for your steadfast love and your faithfulness, for you have exalted above all things your name and your word. On the day I called, you answered me; my strength of soul you increased."*

# REJOICE

# REFLECT

# REACH

WHAT REFRESHED
MY SOUL TODAY?

*"Search me, O God, and know my heart! Try me and know my thoughts! And see if there be any grievous way in me, and lead me in the way everlasting."*

# REJOICE

# REFLECT

# REACH

WHAT REFRESHED
MY SOUL TODAY?

# PSALM 143:8

*"Let me hear in the morning of your steadfast love, for in you I trust. Make me know the way I should go, for to you I lift up my soul."*

# REJOICE

# REFLECT

# REACH

WHAT REFRESHED
MY SOUL TODAY?

## PSALM 145:8-9

*"The Lord is gracious and merciful, slow to anger and abounding in steadfast love. The Lord is good to all, and his mercy is over all that he has made."*

# REJOICE

# REFLECT

# REACH

WHAT REFRESHED
MY SOUL TODAY?

## PSALM 146:5-7

*"Blessed is he whose help is the God of Jacob, whose hope is in the Lord his God, who made heaven and earth, the sea, and all that is in them, who keeps faith forever; who executes justice for the oppressed, who gives food to the hungry."*

# REJOICE

# REFLECT

# REACH

WHAT REFRESHED
MY SOUL TODAY?

*"He heals the brokenhearted and binds up their wounds. He determines the number of the stars; he gives to all of them their names. Great is our Lord, and abundant in power; his understanding is beyond measure."*

# REJOICE

# REFLECT

# REACH

WHAT REFRESHED
MY SOUL TODAY?

## PSALM 147:12-14

*"Praise the Lord, O Jerusalem! Praise your God, O Zion! For he strengthens the bars of your gates; he blesses your children within you. He makes peace in your borders; he fills you with the finest of the wheat."*

# REJOICE

# REFLECT

# REACH

WHAT REFRESHED
MY SOUL TODAY?

*"Let everything that has breath praise the Lord! Praise the Lord!"*

# REJOICE

# REFLECT

# REACH

WHAT REFRESHED
MY SOUL TODAY?

# A NOTE FROM THE AUTHOR
Taylor Deline

Hello new friends!!! I'm Taylor, and I am so excited you're here. A quick bit about me: I live in the Pacific Northwest, I'll never turn down coffee or Thai food, I'm a musical theatre aficionado and I deeply believe in the power of words, both written and spoken. Finally, and most importantly, I have been learning from, walking alongside and loving Jesus most of my life. I am the kind of girl who has MANY jobs, passions, and who over-commits regularly.

Before starting the practice of Sabbath, I experienced burnout multiple times to the point of ending up in the hospital from physical exhaustion, and debilitating anxiety. Beginning the Spiritual discipline of rest has greatly contributed to saving me and that's why this journal was so important for me to create. I pray the Spirit brings you healing, hope, and understanding in ways you don't even know you need.

However you came about this journal, I am so excited that you did, and please know it is not by accident. There is a pursuit and a purpose surrounding you and this journal is just a small part of it. I pray that weekly you experience a deep refresh of your soul. Wherever you may find yourself; overwhelmed, celebratory, apathetic or otherwise…
Jesus will meet you there. If you have followed Jesus for decades or days there is always much to be gleaned from communion with the Spirit.

Thank you to my Kickstarter supporters for showing me that there is true interest behind this project, to my parents Kevin and Sharise who support and inspire me in too many ways to list, and all those listed below in my credits. Thank you from the bottom of my heart for helping make this journal something we can all hold.

Xo, Tay

**Refresh Journal Credits**
*Anela - Copy Editing, Rachel @rlpoems - Poetry*
*Hailey @forthecreative.co - Logo and Brand Design*
*Kadence @kadencecreates - Interior Journal Design*

CPSIA information can be obtained
at www.ICGtesting.com
Printed in the USA
JSHW031204250222
23268JS00006B/129

9 780578 378954